It's Your Future, Plan 4 It!

It's Your Future, Plan 4 It!

Graduate College in 2.5 Years, Get Internships, Pay Off Student Debt, & Plan Ahead For A Bright Future!

Jared S. Taylor

ISBN-13: 9780692846179
ISBN-10: 0692846174

To Mark & Laura Taylor, my parents for raising me right and always being supportive towards whatever it was I was trying to accomplish. Their support and challenges, allowed me to grow into the person I am today.

To Peter & Maureen Taylor, my grandparents for being such a big influence in my life. They taught me that I can truly do whatever I want if I put my mind to it.

To Wendy Dorval, my favorite teacher of all time, that helped transform me into the person I am today. She challenged me and helped develop my mindset to always be "planning ahead."

To Mack Bean, my professor in college for teaching me how I learn best, through his exams and other assignments.

...and to everyone else that I have crossed paths with thus far in my life. My family, colleagues and the many others that I have networked with.

Thank You!

Contents

Introduction

My name is Jared Taylor. I am an ideator, entrepreneur, author, and life coach (okay - so the last two I am currently working towards, but figured for the purpose of the book I would include them both). At the age of twenty-one, I graduated from college with my Bachelor of Science degree in Accounting and Finance in only TWO and a HALF years from Franklin Pierce University in Rindge, New Hampshire. From the time I was a senior in high school until the time I graduated, I had a grand total of FIVE internships. Some of my internships, coupled with a tennis scholarship, and my side business of teaching tennis lessons, helped allow me to pay off my student debt in less than two months after I officially graduated from college. This drive that I had and currently still have, started to show when I was in the sixth grade. It was in this grade that I told my parents that my goal was to get a tennis scholarship to help pay for college. At the time, I had only been playing tennis for about two years, so many people saw that as a major stretch goal. I on the other hand, never saw it as a stretch goal whatsoever. I knew that if I developed a plan, stuck with it and worked hard, the goal would be attainable. My "tennis scholarship" plan looked something like this (in no particular order):

- Stay fit
    - Workout three to five times per week
- Enter tennis tournaments
    - Enter one to two United States Tennis Association (USTA) tournaments each month
- Practice two to three hours per day
    - Work on groundstrokes
    - Work on serves and volleys
    - Hit with other players that were much better than me
- Keep a journal of every match
    - Note my flaws
    - Track my opponent's weaknesses
    - Discuss strategy used
    - Write down the exact score
    - Make note of what needs to be improved upon
    - Offer a line of motivation
- Connect with tennis coaches (once I was allowed to based upon the NCAA rules)

- Use www.berecruited.com to get noticed by college coaches
- Email college coaches and express interest in their programs
- Attend local college matches

Everything in my plan was followed from the time I was in sixth grade, until the time I graduated from high school (May 2012). Perhaps the most important thing that set me apart from other tennis players was the fact that I kept a journal of every one of my tennis matches. Originally, I got the idea from watching Curt Schilling pitch for the Red Sox. After every inning, Curt Schilling could be found in the dugout jotting down notes from the inning he just pitched. Once I began doing so, I loved to take notes on my play and my opponents because 1. It felt great to reflect on the match and 2. It gave me an advantage the next time we played. Essentially, it was a tennis scouting report where I would keep details of what my opponent's weaknesses were, what shots I need to work on and what the score of the match ended up being. This information may not seem useful for people who are not into tennis, but the point is not to focus on tennis players here. The point is to recognize how PLANNING AHEAD IS KEY. Once I got used to planning towards something at a young age, I continued to improve upon the ways that I planned and became obsessed with constantly moving forward in both tennis and life.

My freshman and sophomore year of high school were pretty normal. I was an A and B student who played on the tennis team, had some friends, but generally kept to myself once school was over. I was not a part of any clubs or any other sports at the school. During this time, I focused the majority of my attention towards tennis - I was OBSESSED. I loved the game so much and could not pull myself away from it. Playing tennis for two to three hours per day was not torture, it was a haven. I truly hope everyone, at some point in their life, can be as passionate towards something as I was with tennis. For the most part, things really remained steady for me until about my junior year in high school.

Junior year of high school is a big year for most students. It represents getting more mature and being two years away from applying and going to college (or some other form of education - trade schools, etc.). Typically a person must try and progress as an individual over those next two years - the quicker the better. I really began to see myself improve for the better thanks to a business teacher that I had during my junior year. Her name was Mrs. Dorval. She ended up teaching four or five of the business courses that I chose to take over my junior and senior year. This teacher was different than any other teacher I had come across up until that point. There were several things I liked about her:

- She taught business courses, which I was very into
- She encouraged me to join 2 clubs - FBLA (Future Business Leaders of America) and The Academy of Finance
- Most importantly, she taught me to always think ahead (I took this the most to heart)

Once I had her as my teacher, I began to become much more interested in my studies. I went from being an A and B student, to being a straight A student. Along with that, I began studying up on career paths that really interested me, such as investment banking and private equity. It seemed from this point forward everything began to kind of snowball. I began starting to make connections with professionals who had been in some industry of business throughout their career. I was learning so much about different career paths, and the best part was I was enjoying doing it! Along with getting good grades, making connections, and focusing on my possible career path; my junior year was the first year I started up my tennis lesson business. I had been teaching for a couple of years at that point, so it truly felt like the right time to go off on my own and start getting some of my own clients.

My junior year and senior year both seemed to fly by. By the end of my senior year I had:

- Graduated from the Academy of Finance
- Finished up an Economic Development internship
- Placed first in a local interview competition made up of 80+ high school business students
- Placed second in the NH State Doubles' Tennis Tournament
- Received my PTR (Professional Tennis Registry) certification
- Accepted a tennis scholarship to DII Franklin Pierce University in Rindge, New Hampshire

Many of you reading that last line probably will probably say to yourself "I've never even heard of Franklin Pierce." Well, you wouldn't be the first person to say that. I too never heard of this school growing up and I lived in New Hampshire! I actually ended up learning more about the university through a tennis coach that I used to coach with. At the end of the day, a few things went into my decision to attend Franklin Pierce University:

- It made sense for me financially

There are so many people out there today that know the cost of attending college. They know roughly the amount of debt that they will graduate with, and yet many students still try to attend schools that do not make much sense financially for them. I decided not to be like many of those students. Going to a great school looks very good on a resume, and I urge everyone who can to do so, but only if you can AFFORD IT. Do not put yourself into larger than forty-thousand dollars in debt (if possible) just to get a degree. Go to a school you can afford and make the most out of the opportunity that is in front of you.

- It was approximately one and a half hours from my family

I was always very close to my family growing up. My Mom's side of the family was made up of many aunts, uncles, and cousins (all of my cousins and I were very close in age and were always hanging out with one another). It was important for me to be within a two-hour distance from them in case we wanted to visit one another. I know some students look at colleges with the mindset, "what's the farthest school I can attend?" It's fine if that's part of your agenda, but I am sure that many students would still want to be somewhat close to home (usually within a five-hour drive seems practical).

- It was a small campus

I really liked the fact that less than two-thousand people attended Franklin Pierce University. For me, it meant that in my classes, I would not be "just a number." In many schools that have ten-thousand or more students; classrooms are very large and teachers do not truly know the majority of their students. It was nice to have all of my professors know my first and last name when they saw me.

Overall, prospective college students should take into consideration many of the things I just discussed that swayed my personal college choice. There are more things that can be considered, but at the end of the day, it really all depends on what matters most to you personally. Take a look at everything, because it is YOUR decision.

Up to this point, you are probably thinking that this book is just for prospective college students and maybe underclassman high school students. You would be partially correct. The main reason that I wrote this book was to help students, parents and people of all ages, understand why planning for a bright future is so IMPORTANT. This book is not meant as a complete guide that shows how to plan ahead, but rather as a motivator to get you to start thinking. You are never too young or too old to plan for your future. One of the topics I will tackle the most throughout the book is education, because of how important I believe it truly is. When you read through this book, you may notice some English grammar mistakes. I wrote this book on my own and am not a professional writer. The book was composed how I would speak it to someone in conversation. Throughout it, you will notice how different topics come up several times. The hope is that those topics will be some of your biggest takeaways after reading the book.

Hope you like the book!

If you would like to connect, please visit my website at www.jaredstaylor.com or follow me on Twitter & Instagram @jaredstaylor

CHAPTER 1

My College Years & Strategies

My last two years of high school flew by, and as graduation approached a few things had taken place. I had received a partial tennis scholarship to Franklin Pierce University, had won a local interview competition, graduated from the Academy of Finance (which was an educational program that basically allowed a select few students to gain more finance and accounting insight), and started to build up my resume. The next step in the career process was going off to college and preparing for my career.

College for me began in late August 2012. I was anxious to go off to school, but I was even more anxious to take another step towards my career. I entered Franklin Pierce with almost a semester's worth of credits (twelve credits), thanks to taking numerous "running start" courses while in high school (these running start courses were similar to AP courses, except they were from local and community colleges). It was definitely great to know that even before starting my first day of class, I was already ahead of the game. My first year of school went pretty much the same as any other first-year college student. I made a lot of new friends, ate too much food from the cafeteria, and found out the hard way that 8:00am classes weren't always the best idea. That first year of school went by so quickly and before I knew it, I was saying goodbye to my friends as I got ready to head back home and begin my summer vacation. I was very much looking forward to the summer due to the fact that about a week or two after the semester ended; I received a call that I had received an (unpaid) marketing internship at Capsule Technology, "the leading global provider of medical device information systems and medical device integration solutions for healthcare organizations." Along with that internship, I was also teaching tennis lessons throughout the summer to help pay for school in the fall.

Something Clicked

My sophomore year of college seemed to start off about the same way that my freshman year ended. However, as the end of the fall semester neared, something clicked for me. It was at that point that I decided I would finish school as quickly as possible so I could start my career sooner rather than later. My logic behind this was - would I rather stay in school for the typical four years and accrue large amounts of debt, or would I rather graduate school early, get a good paying job, start paying off my debt sooner, and save up some money all at the same time? The answer was very easy. A lot of my friends and family looked at me as though I were crazy when I told them about how I was going to finish college, but I knew if I fine-tuned a plan and took extra courses over the next six to twelve months, I could definitely do this.

When the spring semester started in January, I was scheduled to take approximately ten classes, totaling approximately twenty-nine credits, through a mix of on-campus and online learning. To put that in perspective, the typical full-time college student takes anywhere from twelve to sixteen credits per SEMESTER, meaning on average that student would take around thirty credits per year. Today, when I look back at the number of courses I took that semester, I can understand and appreciate how some of my friends and family thought I might have been "biting off more than I could chew." Staying on top of the work while getting good grades, playing a collegiate sport, and eating and sleeping the right amount would require a generous amount of self-discipline.

I am happy to say that I was able to handle the heavy course load, but only because I was able to stay SUPER task oriented. My time management skills grew significantly, and I soon realized how much stress my body and mind was able to handle on a daily basis. The only two downsides were that I was not able to see my friends much during that semester, and every minute of the day was essentially utilized to complete school work and play tennis. The upcoming summer would not be much easier. Early on in college, I made it one of my goals to have an internship each summer break during college and that summer would be no different.

Towards the end of the spring semester, I received some great news that Fidelity Investments would like to offer me a co-op position at their Merrimack, New Hampshire location, starting in July, which was about three months after the semester would have ended. This opportunity came about through the use of ALUMNI NETWORKING. At Franklin Pierce there was not an extensive alumni base in business, so I had to really search to find key alumni to connect with. Searching LinkedIn, I was able to find a mutual connection who had attended Franklin Pierce several years before myself. It was at this point that I decided to reach out and ask if she could pass my resume along to someone at Fidelity and see about possible internship opportunities. I was so excited to have earned this opportunity, but was hesitant to accept at first because it would have required me to take the fall semester off from school. Franklin Pierce did not have a co-op program structure like some schools do

- Ex. Northeastern, Wentworth, etc.). My plan meant that instead of finishing school in the fall, I would take a few college courses over the summer and take the fall semester COMPLETELY off and then head back to Franklin Pierce for the spring semester, where I would complete the remaining credits and graduate in May 2015.

After speaking with some faculty and other leadership at Franklin Pierce, I decided that the best move was to accept Fidelity's offer, make some money that summer and fall, then be able to pay for the spring semester in full when I came back to school in January. However, I was not done quite yet. I also decided to accept an (unpaid) Mergers and Acquisition internship at a boutique investment bank (boutique is the term used for an investment bank that typically only works on small deals) in Boston, Massachusetts. I attended the internship for about three months and then informed them that I had accepted a co-op at Fidelity Investments. There were no hard feelings for leaving the internship so soon, but instead, my boss seemed to be happy for the opportunity I had been offered.

Putting It All Together

As you can imagine, my six months at Fidelity Investments went by exceptionally fast. I was able to learn a lot during my time there and I was also able to meet with a lot of great and successful people. It was truly a great opportunity to make connections, gain experience in a field of interest, and add a well-known company to my resume. Although it was an incredible experience, I was looking forward to going back to school to complete my degree and see my friends (who basically had not seen much of me over the last 12 months due to all that was going on).

Right before the spring semester began, I accepted a remote Investment Analyst position at a small venture capital firm in Boston, Massachusetts. I looked at it as another great opportunity to add more experience to my resume and learn from a Harvard MBA graduate (in case you were wondering, that was my boss and owner of the firm). Once again, I became very busy while at school, but still found the time to play collegiate tennis again, see my friends, and do well in school. The semester flew by (like they all did) and before I knew it, I was one month away from graduation when I received an offer to become an Analyst at a boutique investment bank in Manchester, New Hampshire. After much thought, I accepted the job and began counting down the days until I started (which was two days after I graduated from college - I graduated on a Saturday and started work that Monday).

Before I knew it, graduation day had arrived. As I walked up the stage to accept my diploma and officially graduate from college, I began reflecting on my journey to that point. The biggest thing that I took away from that moment, was that it was only the beginning for me, and there was still a lot of work to do to be where I wanted to be in ten to thirty years from now. It all started with PLANNING AHEAD and it will continue with PLANNING AHEAD.

Exactly How I Did It!

I feel it is important to go into more detail about how I was able to graduate with little to no debt and take a crazy amount of courses in a short period of time. I'm sure there are many students wondering how it could be possible for them to follow a similar path. My plan for graduating with low debt and in a fast time period might not be feasible for everyone. The key is to take parts from my plan and utilize them within yours.

One of the most surefire ways to take extra courses while at school, is to go and talk to someone in the Registrar's office at your college or university. I first did this during the fall semester of my sophomore year. I remember going down to the Registrar and asking if I could take some extra classes next semester, since I wanted to graduate early. The kind lady at the Registrar said that I definitely could; however, there would be major extra costs associated with taking additional courses. The way it worked at Franklin Pierce was each student was allowed to take a maximum of sixteen credits per semester without "overloading." If you decided you wanted to go over that amount, there would be a charge of one-thousand dollars per credit, which would mean it would cost a total of three thousand dollars for each extra course (the average course for me consisted of three credits). When I went down to the Registrar's office, I proposed taking an extra three courses during spring semester (along with a standard sixteen credit course load) so you can imagine my disappointment when I found out it would cost me an extra nine-thousand dollars for the semester if I were to take those extra classes through the school.

I am not a person that likes to back down easily. I am a firm believer of not saying the phrase "I can't." The reason being because when we say that phrase to ourselves, it ends up shutting off our brains to the possibility of coming up with ways around something. It is much better to say the phrase "I can" because it enforces a positive mindset and opens our brains to many more possibilities. When I was told by the Registrar's office that there would be a high cost associated with taking extra courses, I began asking a lot of questions to see what my other options could be. After speaking with someone further for thirty minutes or longer, I was finally able to discover my next best option. The option was for me to take extra courses outside of Franklin Pierce. In order to do this, I would need a form titled "Request to Study at Another Institution" (many schools will have similar forms located within the Registrar's office or online). When filling out these forms, there are often some key points to look out for:

- You must attend a regionally accredited school
- You must receive a grade of C or better for the course to count
- Credits will be viewed as transfer credits, therefore they will not count towards your GPA

Many schools will tend to have the above points located somewhere or in some context on their request forms. Also, it is very likely your department Chair and Dean will need to sign off on your forms. Basically, the way that it works is you get the form and figure out which courses would match up well with courses you need to take to fulfill your major, minor or general elective requirements. This is exactly what I did, just on a smaller scale. When I filled out the form, I made sure to fill out many forms to increase my chances of having more courses get approved for me to take at outside universities. Once I found courses that matched up well by doing research online on some local college courses, I was able to fill out my forms completely and submit them for approval.

It differs depending on your school, but the whole approval process only took one or two days for my forms. Once my department Chair signed off on the form, it was sent over to the Dean for her signature. Once I was notified that I was allowed to take the course, I went on to that college's website and registered to take the single course. The beauty of this strategy was that it would typically only cost me about seven to eight hundred dollars to take one of these three-credit courses outside of Franklin Pierce. That equated to a savings of about twenty-two hundred dollars per course. Once I perfected this system, I took course after course outside of Franklin Pierce on top of my standard course-load, during my spring semester and summer semester. The one disadvantage to this strategy is that it often requires some savings up front (if you do not want to take out more loans to execute it). Luckily, I had built up some relatively good savings as a result of being frugal and operating a successful summer tennis business. The clear advantage to using this strategy is the major savings if executed properly. I highly recommend more students use it if they are looking to either graduate a little earlier or save a little money on courses in general.

When I used this strategy, I also arrived at Franklin Pierce with about a semester's worth of credits. This immediately gave me a jump start on graduating early thanks to the fact that I took running start courses during my junior and senior year of high school (running start courses are similar to AP courses and can often give credit for college courses taken in high school). Please take more of a look at one of the major strategies that I used and ask your school today what else you can do if you truly want to graduate early and save money on tuition. It never hurts to ask questions because the worst they can say is NO to whatever you are asking.

I also think it is important to point out the fact that my situation was unique due to the fact that I also received a partial tennis scholarship to Franklin Pierce. This really helped me save money on tuition and thus graduate with less debt.

It is important for every prospective student, current student or parents to look into all the possible ways to save on a college education (assuming you decide to pursue that path). I was able to use a tennis scholarship, my tennis business, internships, strategies and other scholarships to lower my student loan debt and ultimately pay off all of my student loans in less than two months after I graduated from college. Also, another thing that helped me out was Google. Google is incredible - let it be your source for unlimited college savings options!

Other Ways to Save

It's no secret that going to college is usually very expensive for most people. Everyone hopes they get a good portion of tuition paid for through financial aid, but there is often an amount that is up to you to pay. This amount can be low or very high and it is up to you to find ways to lower it. Besides the strategy that I used to graduate college, there are many other ways to save. A few of the other ways are:

- Getting scholarships for writing essays or getting good grades
- Asking your school for ways to save
- Getting into the honors program
- Work-study programs
- Become a research assistant
- Tutor students
- Work at sporting events on-campus
- Sell food on-campus (I used to sell snacks out of my dorm room for double what they cost me to buy)

....and many more ways.

The key when looking for ways to save money on college is to do some research. The above examples are some of the better ways to save, but they are not the only ways. Constantly be researching and finding out what the newest and best ways to save money on college are in your area.

CHAPTER 2

Goal Setting

I FIRST BEGAN working on my plan during my junior year in high school, but plans can be started much earlier or even later on than that. However, the most obvious thing to keep in mind is that the earlier an individual starts a plan, the BETTER.

Set Goals and Set Them Often

In order to have a solid plan, there must first be many goals. Goals are incredible because they often have this magic effect on people in which a goal creates a sense of motivation in an individual. An unmotivated person can often become motivated if they are able to develop some goals. Why is that? It is my belief that when someone sets goals it "paints a picture" in their head of how to achieve that goal and how great it will feel to eventually accomplish it. I've achieved plenty of goals in my life so far, and let me just say that it's a great feeling when you finally accomplish a goal you have been working towards;

whether it has to do with school, sports, fitness, or your life in general, accomplishing goals can make someone feel INCREDIBLE.

In my opinion, there are two different categories of goals. They are:

- Short-term goals – goals with a target accomplish date of three to twelve months
- Long-term goals – goals with a target accomplish date of one to fifty or more years

Also, along with the two categories of goals, I feel as though there are different genres of goals as well:

- Lofty goals – goals that are possible, but are often far-fetched (these goals will be tough to accomplish)
- Realistic goals – goals that are more conservative and have a higher probability of being accomplished (you should always hit these goals)

It is important to note that these goal categories and genres are equally significant. An individual should have a consistent mix of both within their plans. Goals are great to utilize, but make sure that you follow-through with them to the best of your ability. It could be very easy for someone to set one-hundred goals for themselves and foolishly think that they are going to accomplish each and every one of them. Maybe they can though? If that's the case, good for them, but typically people should focus on maybe having five to ten minor and major goals that they have every intention of trying to accomplish.

Develop Solutions to Help Reach Your Goals

It is not enough to just set goals. Solutions must be developed that give an individual the best chance of reaching each one of their goals that they set. What do I mean by solutions? When the term solution comes up, it should be thought of as a rather "straight up" term. A solution in this instance is basically the plan of action to reach your goal. A great example of this "plan of action" could be someone who wants to run a faster mile. Let's say that this individual runs an eight minute mile, but wants to be able to run under a six minute mile in the next six months (it is important to include a time range). The initial solution for most people would probably be to run several times per week to build up the stamina and speed to be able to run a faster mile. Most of the time that solution would probably work, but I personally am not a big fan of the word PROBABLY. Probably in my mind is a term that relates to uncertainty and whenever someone wants to reach a goal, uncertainty should be lowered or eliminated by utilizing precise solutions. A precise solution in this particular example might be for the individual to run long distance three times per week, run short distance two times per week, and in between do exercises to help strengthen their legs so that they are strong enough to generate enough speed to run under a six minute mile with little trouble. Also, it would make sense for the individual to add to the solution even further, thus lowering uncertainty by adding a diet regimen to the plan of action. By adding the diet regimen and the precise exercise schedule to the solution, uncertainty has most certainly been lessened versus what it would have been if the individual just decided to run four days per week in order to work towards their goal. Some people may say that's taking planning to far, but I say when is hedging (lowering) risk ever a bad thing if it leads to more certainty and better results.

Keep Track of Your Goal Progress

Keeping track of your goal progress seems like it would be obvious, but it is still something that many people don't stay on top of. When you keep track of your goal progress, it gives you a constant reminder of the task or objective at hand, and it's that reminder that helps to drive you towards accomplishing that goal. There could most certainly be incidences where someone doesn't track their goals and they are still able to accomplish them, but for the most part people are better off when they track their goals. It goes back to the thought of decreasing uncertainty. By tracking goals either by writing them down on paper, on your computer, on your phone or any other way that seems fitting; it helps to decrease the uncertainty surrounding goal progress and increases the probability that the goal will actually be accomplished.

What Should Your Goals Be About?

It's great to know how to set goals and structure them, but what should your goals even be about. To be honest, that's a pretty open-ended question. A goal can be anything you want it to be. I like to picture a goal as something that I want to accomplish in a set period of time. An example of this could be as simple as making a certain amount of money in a year, winning the state title in your sport, or perhaps becoming a morning person. Goals are more like statements, but questions are often needed along with a goal to determine what the solution could be to reach it. It is important for individuals to always come up with different types of goals because in my opinion constant goal creation increases a person's motivation. Individuals can have any goals having to do with whatever they want, but it is important to have a few that focus on certain areas. The following are examples to consider:

- Monetary-related goals

These are goals that have something to do with money. Money is such an important thing throughout the world. I realize that there are people that say "money isn't everything" and for the most part they would be correct. However, one thing is for certain – money can help solve a lot of issues. Developing goals that are monetary-related is good because it helps people find a solution to gain more money, spend less, or perhaps become more educated on areas such as currency, rates, etc.

- Health-related goals

Health-related goals have something to do with your health and staying fit. People can have opinions about health and fitness, but one thing is for certain; being healthy is never a bad thing. Developing health-related goals is a great way to stay on track and make sure that staying fit and not becoming overweight is a priority.

- Relationship-related goals

These goals have something to do with relationships (which can include personal or professional relationships). When people first hear "relationship" their initial thought is most likely dating-related. Relationship-related goals could have to do with dating and love, but in this particular instance, I am talking more about work-related relationships and connections. A relationship-related goal could be – making a certain amount of connections in a year or connecting one of your connections with another connection.

- Success-related goals

Perhaps the most important type of goal, these typically increase your creativity and help you work towards finding your path towards success. This is my personal favorite type of goal to set. The reason being is because success is what I strive towards. I am always challenging myself with goals related to future success. I believe success-related goals increase a person's chances of actually becoming successful. When success is always on your mind, don't you think that your chances of one day becoming so increase? I believe this to be true. By focusing on success through goals, it can help someone "keep their eye on the prize."

Remember to continuously utilize goals throughout your life and throughout your plan.

CHAPTER 3

Being Proactive, Not Reactive

THROUGHOUT HIGH SCHOOL and college, I observed that there were three kinds of individuals (in regards to planning). The three types of individuals were:

- Forward thinkers
- Consistent doers
- Behind-the-curve slackers (this last one sounds a little harsh, but it's TRUE!)

Forward thinkers are the students that are constantly planning for their future, making connections and taking school seriously (I like to think that I fell into this particular bracket). They are typically good students that are always trying to plan their next move in some shape or fashion.

Consistent doers, on the other hand, are typically individuals that go through the motions in school. They attend their classes, receive relatively good grades and are on the border of becoming forward thinkers if they only thought about the future a little more instead of just the present. A majority of students fall into this category and part of the purpose of this book is to shift more of those consistent doers and behind-the-curve slackers towards becoming forward thinkers.

Behind-the-curve slackers sound a lot worse than they are (although it still is not the best classification). These individuals are the people that decide to either drop out of school, not work hard academically or choose not focus on their future whatsoever. Within this classification, there are many people that simply did (at some point) or do not know what they would like to do in life. This is OKAY! There seems to be many young teens and adults that may not have known what they wanted to do for a career at a young age. Some people are lucky to know what they want to do, and others may need to work harder to figure out what it is exactly that they would like to do. Regardless of what classification a person may fall into, it is important for them to always know what they have control of in their life.

What Do You Have Control Of?

As individuals, it is important that we always realize what we do have control of and what we do not have control of. Growing up, this was somewhat of a difficult concept for me to grasp. I realized early on that I had control of my life and that if I worked hard I could accomplish anything that I wanted to (a theory that I still believe in today). However, there were occasions when I let my height, for instance, bother me when it shouldn't have. For those that have not met me; I am not the tallest person. On a good day, I probably stand somewhere around five feet, six inches. It used to be something that I viewed as a physical flaw that people throughout my life had no problem pointing out or teasing me about. The subject of my height was definitely a sore topic for me for many years. My parents would always respond by saying "You don't have control of your height, so why let it bother you?" Looking back, I can certainly say they were right. It was then that I began to not worry about things that I had no control over.

Once the height thing was behind me, I began focusing further on striving towards success and working out. A lot of people may not know this about me, but I love to workout. I wake up at 4:00am every morning and head off to the gym around 4:30am. It is a great way for me to stay fit, unwind and jump start my day before heading off to work. Focusing on your future and health are two great ways to move past any physical or emotional "flaws" that may bring you down. The earlier someone can adopt this mindset, the better off they will be. It is important to always remember that you have control of your financial situation, you have control of your education, and you have control of your future. There will often be roadblocks that come up with these situations, but typically perseverance and well-thought out planning will trump those obstacles.

What Can You Plan Ahead For?

While in college, this was one of the most important questions I asked myself almost daily. It is a question that can be applied to most situations throughout the day. There are many things you can plan ahead for, here are a few examples:

- There is a big test next week
- Your mortgage is due in a month
- You want to get straight A's this semester
- You want to become a millionaire

All of these examples are things that you can plan ahead for. Now, planning for them may not be easy, but it is possible. This is truly a great point to remember. In life, there are many things that may not be easy to accomplish, but many of those things are possible. Audrey Hepburn said it best when she said: "Nothing is impossible, the word itself says I'M POSSIBLE." Start believing more that anything is possible. By doing this it will help expand your creativity and allow you to become a more positive person. Take a look at some of the great thinkers of the last fifty years. Bill Gates, Steve Jobs, Elon Musk and many more tackled issues and areas that many considered "impossible." Instead of thinking many of the issues that needed solving were impossible, people like Gates, Jobs, and Musk tackled issues by being positive that they could find solutions through creativity and perseverance (and they SUCCEEDED!).

Individuals should make lists of what they should plan for as early as possible. Why does starting early matter? Starting early allows people to "get ahead of the game." Think of it this way; when is it ever bad to be fifteen minutes early for an interview? The answer is, it's never bad to be fifteen minutes early for an interview, so why should goals and other things that you can plan for be late? Plan early, plan often, ignore what you can't control, and you will almost certainly be in a better position than most because of that mindset.

What Connections Can You Make Now?

There is a good chance that most people have heard the phrase "it's all who you know." That was a phrase that I use to draw upon early on. It was part of what led me to ask myself what connections I could make now? I asked myself this question almost daily and thanks to the social networking site, LinkedIn; connecting with anyone became a lot easier. I made connections through a combination of LinkedIn, emails (via Gmail), phone calls, and in-person meetings. Obviously, the best type of meeting a person can set up is an in-person one, however, conversations via email and phone calls are nothing to dismiss either. It is important to ask yourself "what connections can you make now?" Expanding your network is always necessary when moving forward in life. I don't care if you think your network is big enough already. If that's the case then good, but there is always room for you to expand your connections. Find mutual connections and reach out to them to learn more about their career, and about their current role. Mutual connections are the easiest people to connect with, since you share a mutual friend or colleague. Having a mutual connection certainly makes the initial conversation a lot easier. Other possible connections can include:

- People that work at your current company that you are not familiar with
- People that work at a company you want to work with
- Influential people that you would love to learn from (if possible)

- Random connections on LinkedIn that you have common interests with (I would advise you use this strategy with caution)

Remember to always make connections. Strangers are only people you have not connected with. It is great to connect with people at different stages of your life, but it is easiest to make connections the younger you are. High school students, college students, and recent graduates can in many cases have an easier time connecting than older people can. Why is this? It seems as though when a young person reaches out to someone who is established, the person assumes that they only want to learn (which is often true). When someone older reaches out to someone who is successful (more so than them), it could seem like they definitely want something. Of course, the assumption could be wrong and it really all depends on different situations.

CHAPTER 4

Connections Are Important

DURING THE COURSE of high school and college, making connections was one of my favorite things to do; it also helped that I was quite good at it (sorry if that sounds cocky). I do not care what career path you decide to go into, but one thing is for certain; making connections is important all the time! I think one of the main reasons that I liked doing so was because of the fact that I am a people person at heart. Growing up, I always loved talking with people and getting to know more about what they do. Those two qualities certainly helped me make better connections as I got older.

One of the biggest reasons why some people choose not to connect with certain people is because it is sometimes perceived that they want something. If you want to connect with a multi-million dollar real estate investor, for example, be sure to let them know that you would like to speak with them to learn more about their career, how they got to where they are today, and perhaps what advice they have for you as you begin your real estate career. Now this is just an example, but those points are key. When I was making all of my connections over the years, there were three main things I wanted to take away from a connection:

1. I wanted to learn more about their career.
2. I wanted to understand more about how they got to where they are today.
3. I wanted to hear what advice they had for me.

What you takeaway could be different from what I was looking for out of a connection, but those three should be your core focus when meeting with a potential new connection. I was able to make hundreds of connections over the years by being polite, persistent and utilizing current connections to make more connections. Remember, it takes money to make money and it takes connections to make more connections. You can never have enough, so be sure to always be on the lookout for networking events, job fairs (go even if you aren't looking for a job), and any other situations you feel will allow you to make more connections down the road.

Never Turn Down a Networking Opportunity

Websites like www.meetup.com and www.eventbrite.com are great for finding "ideal" networking events. These websites let you search for events based on exactly what you are looking for. For example, if you are interested in attending a real estate event, search for that within the website and voila! Another good source of finding networking events is through your college's alumni network. There is a good chance that your college or university throws events around your area from time to time. These networking events are great because even if you do not know anyone, more than likely it will be a warm gathering due to the fact that everyone there at some point went to the same school as you. After all, alumni need to look out for one another right? I made connections with a few of the top alumni at my school while I was still attending Franklin Pierce. Most alumni are more than willing to help out any past, current or future students.

As you look for networking opportunities, there may be some that you feel the need to pass on. Before doing so, ask yourself a few questions:

- Why do I not feel this is worth going to?

Try to really focus in on this. If the best answer you can come up with is that your friend is having a few people over; then chances are that is not a good enough reason to pass on a potentially valuable networking event.

- If I attend, how will I make sure I get something out of it?

It is important for you to already know the type of people that will most likely be attending a specific event. Once you know who may be attending, be sure to already have some conversation starters ready and questions to ask. Ideally, you want to try to speak with everyone there and make lasting connections. The hope is that one connection will turn to three, and so on. I had a lot of success connecting with people and turning those connections into even more connections thanks to introductions. It is very important to ask your current connections who they think would be another good source or person for you to connect with.

Some of the events that you come across or decide to attend may have a cost associated with them. For instance, it will sometimes cost money to attend an entrepreneur networking event or a hackathon. Weigh that cost thoroughly and see if there is a good return on investment. Is it worth your time and money to attend? Chances are it will be, and in at case, sign on up (although some events are pricey)!

LinkedIn Is Your Best Friend

There may be a few people that laugh at the sub-title of this section. The reason I refer to LinkedIn as a "best friend" is because you should know the ins and outs of it (much like you should know a lot about your best friend). LinkedIn is great because it allows you to see all of your connections in one place with a sort of "Facebook-like" feel to it. You get to see someone's background, profile picture, interests and contact information. My favorite part of LinkedIn is the fact that I can almost always see who my current connections are connected with. Now, I could just reach out to that particular person myself, but chances are they will not respond since we "technically" do not know each other. The best way to handle this situation is to reach out to your current connection and ask for an introduction. A nice way to word it could look like this:

> Hi [First Name],
>
> Hope all is well. I noticed that you're connected with [First Name] [Last Name]. How do you two know one another? I was hoping that you could introduce me to [First Name]. It would be great to learn more about their background and career path. I would really appreciate it.
>
> Thanks,
> [Your First Name]

Email Conversations Are Nice; Phone Calls and In-Person Visits Are Better

There are three main avenues that a person can utilize to network with someone:

1. Email
2. Phone Calls
3. Face-to-Face

Each is very useful, but the best form of networking still has to be face-to-face. When you are face-to-face with someone it allows you to see someone's personality. It is very easy to act differently through email and phone calls, but when you are face-to-face, it puts each party on the spot and makes them have to be much more real with one another.

Stay in Touch

It's great to make connections, but how many people actually stay in touch with ALL of their connections? My guess is that that number is not too high. This is a great opportunity for you to stand out from the crowd. I highly suggest that you stay in touch with the connections that you make. That does not mean if you have five-hundred connections that you should be checking in with them every few months to see how they are doing. In all honesty, it would be pretty counterproductive to do such a thing. However, what you should be doing is keeping in touch with between twenty-five and fifty of your biggest or closest connections. It shows that you care and it lets you stay in tune with what they are working on, who they are connecting with and what new advice they may have for you. It is important to always be looking for more advice from your connections. Advice is something that you can never get enough of. The more, the better! Almost ninety-nine percent of your connections will be more than willing to provide sound advice when possible, so definitely ask.

The irony here is that even though it is so important to stay in touch with your connections, it is really tough to do so! Work, extracurricular activities and sometimes school gets in the way of crucial follow-ups that often do not get to take place. You truly need to make a point of touching base with past connections every few months. One of the best ways to do so is through leaving yourself notes or adding reminders on your calendar. I personally will just go through my LinkedIn contact list and try to touch base with some of my contacts every few months. I probably should utilize a reminder, but thus far I have just committed it to memory that I need to do it every few months. No matter what industry you decide to go into, connections will play a huge role. Ever hear the saying "it's all who you know?" Well, there is some truth to it. Connections, combined with hard work, a winning attitude, and a good track record can make a person never have to worry about finding a job, should they decide to leave their current employment or start up a new enterprise.

Remember that making connections can also be fun and very worthwhile. When I was interning at a top financial firm while I was in college, I made sure to meet with a ton of people, but more importantly I made sure to make the experience fun and to gain a lot from these meetings. During that internship, I was able to connect with more people than the other interns had for sure. It was getting to the point where I was connecting with two people or more per day. Luckily, I was only twenty years old at the time, which is one of those ages where people will tend to make time to connect with you and teach you whatever they can. Some people may find this bad, but I feel it is very important to use age to your advantage. If for some reason you are older, please do not let that discourage you from making connections. Instead, explain yourself to possible connections so that age becomes an afterthought (this is only the case when possible connections may feel you want something besides knowledge from them - watch out for this!).

CHAPTER 5

Side Jobs = More Cash

EARLIER ON IN the book, I mentioned how throughout high school, college and even today, I have a side business of teaching tennis lessons. Teaching tennis helped me pay for school, become a better tennis player and build up my savings. Also, it kept me busy on weekend mornings and some weeknights. I am so happy that I started teaching tennis at a young age, for it has allowed me to create a nice side business as a result of the work I have put into it. Today, I even run the local parks and recreation tennis program throughout the summer. In this program, I teach adults and children of all ages the game of tennis. Teaching tennis was not the only side job or business that I have had.

When I graduated college, tennis was not the only avenue in which I earned side income. Several months after graduation, I actively searched AngelList (www.angel.co) - a website where established and early-stage startups show who they are to the world. On this site, many startups also post internships and jobs that they are looking to fill. From an early age, I have always been interested in startup companies so I thought working for one would be quite the experience. I used AngelList a little differently than most people did. I would not search the job boards because of the heavy competition from other applicants (not because I thought I didn't stack up, but rather, why would I even want to compete with hundreds of resumes?). If you log onto AngelList you will see that for certain jobs there are anywhere from sixty to one-hundred or more applicants. I consider myself a quality candidate, but I will not waste my time applying for jobs that have that kind of applicant traffic. I decided to put my networking skills to work. I would sift through the thousands of startups that interested me, regardless if they were hiring or not. From there, I would reach out to the founders of the company via LinkedIn or email and ask to connect with them to learn more about their company and discuss with them how I could become a part of what they are doing on a part-time, remote basis. It was interesting to see how many founders were open to connecting with me. Most of the companies that I was connecting with were not even looking for new employees or part-time, remote workers. It was my job to sell them on the value that I could bring to their startup (even on a part-time basis).

Finally, after reaching out via LinkedIn and email (and speaking with many startup founders), I landed with a startup that was willing to use me part-time for a relatively fair hourly rate. The opportunity consisted of only about four to six hours of work per week, and was truly a great way to generate some income along with my full-time job and tennis business. Some of the best things about this part-time job was the fact that the team valued my input, it was remote, and I was learning a lot and making money all at the same time. After about three or four months someone at the company decided to leave (it was a small team) so they asked me if I could pick up extra hours. I happily agreed and picked up the extra hours and welcomed the extra income. After another two to three months another employee decided to leave. It turns out this employee was pretty integral (as was the other one who left). The Chief Executive Officer (CEO) again came to me and asked if I could work extra hours, which I once again replied - YES! This time, the hour increase came with a new title which was the "Head of Customer Success." The title really didn't speak to what I was doing though, and in all reality, probably a more appropriate title should have been the "Director of Operations" instead. With this new position, I had much more responsibility and was working about twenty or more hours per week, on top of my full-time job and teaching tennis. Eventually, it came to the point that if you called the company's main line, it would actually direct to my cell phone. It was certainly difficult to manage all that was going on, but the extra money took my mind off the whole situation. I was money hungry and that is all that mattered to me.

CHAPTER 6

Time Management is Key

One of the skills I am most proud of is my time management. From a young age, I learned that time should be valued like money. Unfortunately, taking on more money making activities typically means that there is less time. This is okay. The key to less time is learning to manage it properly. I personally do not think schools spend enough time teaching students about time management. Sure, some schools try to instill time management into students at an early age, but from my point of view, they have failed. Time management is so important for an individual to master if they want to be successful. Everyone should want to put more on their plate and not let time be a crutch in the process. Wouldn't you like to do more? Well, more than likely you can and it all comes down to how you are managing your time.

When's the last time you did a time analysis? A time analysis is when you break down what a typical day looks like from an hour or minute perspective. I frequently implement a time analysis to make sure I am spending my time wisely and to see where I can create more time in my schedule. Here's an example:

Jared's Daily Time Analysis (Current)

Sleep = 8 hours
Gym = 1 ½ hours
Commuting = 1 hour (I live close to the gym and work)
Reading = 1 hour
Work = 9 hours
Writing = ½ hour
Miscellaneous = 2 hours
Remaining time = 1 hour per day

Here's another example of a time analysis (this is what my time analysis looked like when I was teaching tennis, working my full-time job and working at the startup company on a part-time basis):

Sleep = 7 hours
Gym = 1 ½ hours
Commuting = 1 hour
Work = 8 hours (full-time job)
Tennis = 1 hour
Startup = 4 hours
Miscellaneous = 1 ½ hours
Remaining time = 0 hours per day

As you can see in the second example, there was no free time for me during those several months when I was juggling three jobs. This was a very stressful time for me, but I was truly able to manage it all, thanks to managing my time properly (and in most cases to the minute). I advise everyone to conduct a time analysis of themselves every few weeks. It is such a useful tactic and will let you know where you are spending the bulk of your time and where you may be able to save time.

Keeping Track

Another useful time management tactic that I used often in college and high school were checklists. I loved checklists because all I needed was a pen and paper. At the end of class or during class, I would write down what I needed to get done that night (or in some cases that week). Then, I would occasionally even write down next to it how long I thought the task would take me. This was great because it showed I was already thinking ahead and thus preparing my brain for what was about to come. Also, utilizing checklists allowed me to prioritize assignments ahead of time, rather than waiting until the last minute to see what needed to be done quickly. Now for those of you who do not want to write out a checklist, certainly feel free to utilize technology if you would prefer. You could use your phone, a tablet or a laptop to type out checklists (you could even print it if you wanted a hard copy to hold onto or hang up somewhere). Once I wrote out my checklists, I would always fold them and stick them in my back pocket so that I could pull it out and add to it very quickly and easily. Checklists were a great tool in helping me stay focused and manage my time appropriately.

White Board It

Another useful tool that I used to love to use was a white board. In college, I would hang a whiteboard next to my desk and write all sorts of deadlines and schedules on it so I knew what was due and when I was supposed to be somewhere. Combining the whiteboard notes and my checklists really helped me manage my time exceptionally well. It used to be so refreshing to come back to my dorm after class or tennis practice, sit down and look at both my checklist and whiteboard to see what needed to get done. The one big tip with whiteboards I can give you is to make sure you also keep due dates and tasks somewhere other than your whiteboard. It is possible for someone to accidentally erase what you wrote (believe me, it happened all the time in college). Always have a backup plan for the notes that you leave yourself on your whiteboard.

CHAPTER 7

Handling Stress

In college, I placed a lot of stress upon myself. The bulk of it was due to taking an obscene amount of classes in a semester, while also playing a collegiate sport. I am happy to say that I was able to handle this and became very productive as a result of it. Some people would most likely argue that it is not good for a college student to place a lot of stress upon themselves. One reason is because it is not good for your health. Another reason is because it can sometimes hurt performance in work or school. I agree that a lot of stress can often result in negative consequences, but also feel as though (when dealt with correctly); it allows an individual to focus in on what they are trying to accomplish and pushes them to actually complete whatever that objective or task is.

You Will Face Stress In Your Life, Why Not Practice?

Stress often makes people act differently than they would be without it. I believe there are two types of stress: good stress and bad stress (I know, obvious right?). Now many health professionals may say that is incorrect, all types of it are bad for your health and they may be right, but it's sometimes needed to reach your goals. Stress is what places that feeling upon you that makes you say "I need to do this and do this now." How many of you have placed stress upon yourself during school or work at some point? My guess is that if we were all in an auditorium 99% of people would be raising their hands after that question was asked. Since it is often inevitable, my view on it was always to use it to my advantage.

In high school, I did not face too much of it (unless it was tennis-related). However, in college, I faced stress as a result of juggling a collegiate sport, my heavy course load, and other activities. I approached stress head on by creating a plan that dealt with it. The plan looked like this:

- Get a decent amount of sleep
    - It's college, so the traditional 8 hours was often hard to come by.
- Deal with schoolwork first
    - When schoolwork is completed, life becomes a little less stressful.
- Make some time for friends
    - This is something I did early on in college, but drifted away from slightly during my

insane junior year spring semester with twenty-nine credits.

- Make sure to exercise
    - o Working out is one of the surefire ways to make sure your stress levels stay in check.

Reduce Stress with Exercise & Activities

I love playing tennis and working on business-related activities, but along with those two things I absolutely love working out. I got into working out during college with one of my friends that lived in my dorm building. Ever since then, I have tried to work out a few days a week. Today, I wake up every morning at 4:00am and head to the gym for 4:30am. Getting up out of bed early and off to the gym is one of the best ways for me to lower my stress levels and prepare for the day. It also makes me feel good and full of energy. My workout will typically always be a body specific workout (one day is back and biceps, chest and triceps, etc.) and I try to mix in a few days of cardio each week as well. Here is where a lot of people go wrong when it comes to working out in my opinion:

1. They will not workout at all.
2. They will only run.
3. They will only lift.
4. They workout longer than an hour.
5. They workout less than an hour.

It is important to go to the gym (leave the phone in your bag – do not be that person that is on their phone the whole time), workout for an hour and get back to whatever it is you'd be doing if you were not at the gym.

How to Utilize Stress for Better Performance & Productivity

People reading the headline for this section are probably saying "Is this guy crazy?" No, I am not crazy, but I do feel stress (when utilized properly) can help people perform better and help lead to more accomplishments. Throughout my life, I have used what I call "positive stress" to help myself get things done. When I was younger, I would use this to help me get prepared for big tennis matches. Then as I got older and was in college, I would utilize positive stress to help me get prepared for exams, write papers, do homework and take a lot of courses all at once. Today, I use it to do a good job at work, thus setting myself up for future promotion opportunities. Go ahead and use stress to your advantage, just make sure it is the positive kind. Negative stress is stress that is not needed because it comes about from worrying about things you can't control. An example could be a tree falling on you when you are driving, or getting a bad grade on an exam after you have already taken it. Those are two things that are out of your control so do not dwell over them.

Key Stressful Issues

There are many stressful issues that a person will face throughout their life. Perhaps some of the most stressful events happen early on for most people. Getting into a good college, doing well in college, graduating college to have a chance at a bright career, getting that first job to help propel your career and planning your career path accordingly so that you can set yourself up for a bright future. The truth of the matter is, while there are many things that come to mind that are clearly stressful events; most people will agree that many events could become stressful based on different situations. Almost ANY event can be stressed over. The key is to try and not stress over certain events. Should you be stressed about an exam or a deadline at work? Yes. Should you be stressed about a big speech that is coming up or an important interview? Yes. Should you stress over laundry that needs to be done or what you will eat for dinner? No.

CHAPTER 8

Formalizing A Plan

PLANNING AHEAD IS great and so is thinking about a plan for the future, but many people may ask themselves "How Do I Start My Plan?" A plan can differ depending upon the person, so there truly isn't a one stop shop for what your plan should look like. I can comment on the way that I formalized my personal plan that allowed me to continuously hit the goals that I set up for my life. Also, it should be noted that plans differ based upon what stage someone is at in their life. When I was originally coming up with my plan, I was about a junior or senior in high school. In my opinion, this is probably the best time in someone's life for them to start thinking about their plan. However, it is not uncommon for someone at that age to be unsure about their future. Formulating a plan at a young age is recommended whenever possible.

What Should It Include?

Plans can vary depending on the person it is for, the stage of someone's life or perhaps other reasons.

The key is just having one and shaping it to be similar to someone who has had success with their own plan. When I was formulating mine several years ago, I started with researching where I wanted to go to school. The reason I started there was because I was a junior in high school preparing to go to college soon. When looking at schools, I made sure to look for schools that made the right sense financially and that would give me an opportunity to succeed upon graduating.

The next steps in my plan actually did not start coming to fruition until my freshman or sophomore year of college. It was at this point I began looking at ways to shave off time so that I could graduate college in only two and a half years with my undergraduate degree, versus the traditional four-year degree that most people pursue. Whether you are in the same boat as I was or have a different situation, the point still remains that it is important to include ways that you can shave off time from traditionally long processes. Remember, time is precious and can be used for more important tasks that can help get you ahead of this game we call LIFE.

Within your plan, it is important to include ways to save time on certain things. Make sure that your plan also includes vital things like possible career paths, ideal connections, and additional ways of learning and investment or saving ideas. The crazy thing is that many people never think of any of these things. The key is to think about these things early and often. When I began my plan I wanted to become an investment banker. I decided this early in my senior year of high school. It was at that time I began researching more about what an investment banker does, discovered what relevant contacts I could learn from and connect with within the industry. Also, what would be my plan of action to eventually land a good investment banking job out of college? It was a lot to think about at the time, but I was so happy that I did because it prepared me for the difficult journey. I'm not sure if many people know what it takes to become an investment banking analyst, but it is no picnic. It requires great attention to detail, a strong work ethic, the ability to deal with high volumes of stress and the right connections (also being a Microsoft Excel ninja helps as well!).

The best part of my whole process was making numerous connections. Most of the connections that I made in the industry became almost like mentors to me. They would hop on calls with me and tell me about their day-to-day tasks, and discuss what I would need to do if I really did want to break into the industry upon graduation. It was at this point I knew that a school like Franklin Pierce University was not going to make me easily stand out. I needed to be creative, persistent and super goal driven. I chose for the next step in my plan to take many college credits to allow me to graduate early, to save money, and have a good job waiting for me prior to graduation.

Now that we have discussed that your plan should typically include school and career research and relevant connections; it is time to discuss why it is important for your plan to also include short-term goals, long-term goals, more research, time-lines, side income ideas, and education tools. Many of you are probably asking, what am I even talking about here? Education tools? Huh? Don't worry, I will explain what I mean by each of these soon. In the meantime, let's dive more into the overall plan.

Short-term and long-term goals (we discussed these early on in the book, but I feel it is important to revisit them again in a slightly different light) are so important for an individual's development. Short-term goals should be ones that are attainable within a period of anywhere from one day to one year (or even sooner in some cases). While long-term goals, on the other hand, are often ones that are attainable within a period of one or more years (meaning you could have a long-term goal with an end date of fifty years in the future). The key word here is "attain-able." Attainable goals are ideal because it means the individual actually has a shot to hit them. This is very important because a goal that is not attainable and perhaps does not have a timeline, is really not a goal at all, it's just a dream. Dreams are great, but let's be honest, so many people in the world dream, but so many never go the extra mile and accomplish what they are capable of. Goals are so important because they help keep us on track. They can be used in sports, education, work, and so much more. There really is no limit to the amount that a person can set. As mentioned earlier, it is so important to make sure that you have a good mix of short-term and long-term ones that hit upon certain issues that have to deal with things like money, life, your career and your future plans in general.

Next, it is time to conduct more research (many of you are probably sighing because after all research is often long and boring - I beg to disagree!). Research can be your best friend in many situations, because it allows you to become more knowledgeable on a certain subject or interest. When I was a senior in high school, I didn't really have any idea what an investment banker did throughout their day-to-day. It was research and making high-quality connections that allowed me to learn more about what occurs on the job, and how I could prepare to break into the industry.

Timelines tend to go hand in hand with goal setting. Everyone should put timelines on certain issues like retirement, buying a home, buying a second home, taking a vacation, going back to school, etc.

Timelines plus goals, are truly a great combination. They allow individuals to begin thinking in more depth about certain things. Without timelines and goals, there is not much order. I urge everyone to think about what they can apply timelines to, because the earlier you figure that out, the better off you will be.

How many people focus on just their job and that is it? Chances are, many of you will answer yes to this question. It seems as though many people are okay with the typical "9-to-5" job. Then, they leave and go home, only to relax or do something else. Then, when it comes to weekends they socialize or do other things as well. What people fail to do is calculate how many hours they have left after things like work, sleep, eating, commuting, and much more. It is important to do this simple calculation every so often, to look into where your time is being spent and how you could potentially spend it much better. Do you really need that twenty-minute shower? Is watching television two hours per night a good use of your time? It is questions like these that will allow you to shed time off of unnecessary tasks and spread it out amongst more "high priority" ones. Depending on if you are able to carve out a significant amount of time; you should consider ways to create side income for yourself. Side income is a great way to save up extra money, pay off unwanted debts or perhaps invest more easily. My whole life, tennis has been my number one side income source. I am so happy to have played tennis because it was able to reward me with a tennis scholarship, but more importantly, it allowed me to create some significant side income for myself. Along with tennis, I have also had many other side income "hustles" that brought in some extra money. One of my favorite side income jobs, was working for a San Francisco Bay area startup company. I am from New England, so I was able to make the hours work. At my peak, I was working approximately twenty hours per week at this "side hustle." I was a 1099 employee here, where I was the "Head of Operations/ Customer Success." I learned a lot, and was able to make some money as well. It was a truly great experience. The way I was able to make it work, was by planning the way my time was spent to the second. My schedule at the time looked something like this:

- Wake up at 5:00am EST.
- Go to the gym.
- Shower, eat breakfast and go to work.
- Start work at 8:00am EST.
- Work until 5:30pm EST.
- Start my side job at 3:00pm PST.
- Work until 7:00pm PST.
- Go to bed at 10:00pm EST.
- Do it all over again Monday through Friday.

On the weekends my schedule would include teaching approximately ten to sixteen hours of tennis lessons and working some hours at my side job. It was very stressful and I always needed to make sure I did not get off track, but the money was good and I was able to save up a lot over the course of one year (the amount of time I was at the side job before I left).

It is important to think of good side income streams that are out there for you. What are you good at? Should you start your own side business or should you work for someone else? Is freelancing an option? There are many questions that you can ask yourself to determine what could be the best side income avenue for you. One thing is for certain though and that is to FIND some sort of side income job or source. College debt, medical bills, real estate investments, etc. can all be paid for simply by utilizing your "side income streams."

Another important thing for you to include in your plan is educational resources and tools. The key thing to remember is that you should never stop learning. Knowledge is so important and utilizing things like free online courses and books can do wonders for someone. I personally have learned more by reading many books and taking free online courses, than I did attending college. The reason being, because I was studying solely what interested me. Online courses on sites like Coursera (www.coursera.com)

and Udemy (www.udemy.com) are great for learning a variety of skills and subjects. I have used Coursera to get several certificates on Entrepreneurship from the University of Pennsylvania - Wharton School of Business. If you feel like reading books will help you learn more, then by all means, gravitate towards that. Please do not forget to make a list of all the books you would like to read. If you feel overwhelmed by writing and researching all the books and putting them on paper, go ahead and use a free resource like Goodreads (www.goodreads.com), which allows you to organize and research the ones that you would like to read. The site also lets you track your reading progress, along with many other features. Now that you know more about the resources that are out there - start learning more TODAY!

Put It on Paper (or On Your Computer)

You don't have to actually put your plan on paper or on your computer if you do not want to, but it's the ideal action to take. Writing or typing out your plan allows you to hold yourself accountable to following it throughout your journey. There will be times that you differ from it and that is okay, but most of the time you should stick with what you originally put down. Many successful startup companies have pivoted throughout their journey to success, so it is possible you may decide to pivot from your plan, and that is okay. It is important to not veer too far off the path.

When I was creating my plan, I originally just left it to memory. Then after thinking about it for a while, I decided to start writing it down on paper. Once I wrote my goals down and my plan in general, I began to notice that I was following it more. It was great to wake up every morning and see that it was always right there in front of me (please make sure to glance at your plan every day - trust me it helps). Looking over your plan every day keeps your "eye on the prize." Being motivated is half the battle when it comes to executing your plan to the fullest. That is why, it is important to constantly know what you are trying to accomplish.

Develop a Strategy

Developing a strategy basically, goes hand in hand with your plan. Along with keeping track of it, it's important to create the best strategy that will ultimately give you the most value towards hitting the main points of what you are following. When I was working on mine, my main strategy was to focus on the connections piece of it. After all, most people love to use the phrase "it's all who you know." I go into more detail about how important connections are, no matter what industry you decide to go into. Being well connected is never going to hurt you. The reason that

I focused on connections specifically, was because I was trying to break into the investment banking industry. For those of you that are unfamiliar with this industry, it is often difficult to "join the club." I felt that making connections and genuinely trying to learn from professionals in the industry, would be the best way for me to increase my chances of getting an investment banking job (and it worked!).

Have a Timeline

One of the biggest mistakes people can make is not applying timelines onto everything they do. I view timelines and goals almost in the same category because of how important they both are. There really are so many things that you should be applying them to. Here are a few important ones:

- Short-term goals
- Long-term goals
- Your education
- Your career
- Your future

Some of these items are obvious, but the whole point of bringing each one of these up is to stress the importance of them. I was a huge fan of timelines in my journey, and am still a big fan of them today. They help me stay focused and give me a way of tracking my progress, so that I can tell myself to either slow down or pick up the pace to accomplish what I am trying to do.

Start Following It!!!

We discussed that often in a plan, it is important to include many different things. However, all of those things truly mean nothing unless we are able to apply some action to start following them. It is a shame when someone plans, and then fails to succeed on what they set out to do. Not acting on a plan is just as bad as not planning. A good way to make sure you are staying on track, is to tell people about what you are trying to accomplish. This way, the possibility of them "coming down hard on you " increases, if you are not following what you said you said you would do. I know that if I tell my friends or family I am going to do something and I do not, they will constantly be letting me know that I'm failing (this isn't a shot at my friends and family – I actually LOVE that they do this). Even though it probably shouldn't, knowing that I potentially let people down does not sit well with me. I want people to know that I am working hard and following the path that I have set out for myself. Benjamin Franklin said it best, when he said "Well done is better than well said." That is a quote I always try to follow.

CHAPTER 9

Never Stop Learning

GROWING UP, I always liked school, but I never loved it. I believe that was partly due to the fact that I had to study certain subjects that were not appealing to me, like science (if you're into science I mean no disrespect, but it wasn't my cup of tea). My favorite subjects in high school and college all followed a similar theme; they had something to do with business. Courses with a focus in business were what I loved to learn about. I did not care too much for the other subjects, but it was still my responsibility to make sure that I studied for those courses so that I could receive good grades. Even if you do not like certain courses when you're in high school and college, please do not let that stop you from doing well in them. I am a big believer in the fact that grades aren't everything, however, all classes should still be taken very seriously, with the intention of getting the best grades possible.

Whether You're in School or Out of School, Take Advantage of Learning

The beauty of college is that most of the time you get to study only what you would like to. A typical exception to this rule, is if you go to a Liberal Arts college or university. Even when you attend one, there are still much more courses that focus on what you like to study, depending on what you choose your major to be. The biggest thing to remember with learning, is that even though you graduate college (or whatever other form of education or trade you decide to pursue after high school), it does not mean that learning has to stop. There are opportunities for you to go back to school and get your masters, or perhaps join a certificate program. The options are out there for further education, it is up to you to go out and "grab them!" For those that take advantage of the options available, you may be considered a "constant learner." I am a big believer in constant learning. I define it as, the art of consistently trying to learn new skills and things that interest you.

Learning Opportunities

Constant learning should be executed by everyone no matter what they do or one day will do for a living. When is learning a new skill a bad thing? When is mastering a current skill a bad thing? The answer to both questions is, never! Learning is a great and beautiful thing that I believe many people in the world take for granted. The beauty of learning in today's society, is that there are so many options for which we can learn. Today, we can learn through videos, podcasts, books, infographics and many other options. My personal favorite ways to learn are through books, videos, and podcasts (which I mentioned earlier). One of the reasons that I love to learn through books is because there are so many great ones. The options are truly limitless! I can read ones that are very old or newer ones that are relevant to the times. Videos are great because they give me a visual and a sort of classroom-like feel, when learning. Then, there are podcasts, which come in handy when I am on the go. All I do is download a certain podcast on my phone and BAM - I have something to listen to on my commute.

Online Courses Entrepreneurs Will Love

Even though I consider this book to be for EVERYONE, there is a certain place in my heart for entrepreneurs. I thought it would be a good idea to include some of the online courses that (focus on entrepreneurship) I believe people of all ages should look into. After all, even if you have ZERO interest in business, it is still something everyone should look into at some point down the road. Entrepreneurial skills would be a great addition to anyone's skill set.

I have always been a big fan of online courses (anytime there is a way to learn new skills, it's great). Websites like Coursera, Udemy, Codecademy (www.codecademy.com) and many more, are great for learning some new skills or adding to ones you already possess. Online courses are great for anyone, but I decided to single out entrepreneurs in this section (as mentioned above) due to the large selection of entrepreneurial courses readily available. Below is a list of some courses (via Coursera) entrepreneurs should seriously take a look at:

Entrepreneurship Specialization (University of Pennsylvania, Wharton School of Business)

- A specialization on Coursera is a group of courses, rather than just one course. The Entrepreneurship Specialization covers topics such as Developing the Opportunity, Launching Your Start-Up, Growth Strategies, Financing and Profitability, and a Capstone Project. It's definitely a GREAT option for people looking to learn more about the entrepreneurial process. I completed this specialization and let me just say that it was FANTASTIC! The videos, quizzes, and the final capstone project are great ways to help you expand your horizons and learn more about entrepreneurship from a great university.

How to Finance and Grow Your Startup - Without Venture Capital (University of London & London Business School)

- I believe that every entrepreneur would be interested in learning more about this topic. Growing your startup without venture capital (also known as "bootstrapping") is crucial for entrepreneurs because it allows them to keep more of their company and ultimately increases the chances of a higher valuation if they succeed.

Successful Negotiation: Essential Strategies and Skills (University of Michigan)

- Negotiation is crucial whether you are an entrepreneur or a consumer buying a car. This is yet another essential course that will help you develop a necessary entrepreneurial and life skill.

How to Start Your Own Business Specialization (Michigan State University)

- The setup of this specialization is slightly similar to the specialization offered by Wharton. In this specialization, students will learn about topics like: Developing an Entrepreneurial Mindset, The Search for Great Ideas, Planning, Structure, Strategy, and a Capstone Project that deals with Action.

Entrepreneurship: Launching an Innovative Business Specialization (University of Maryland)

- This is a very in-depth specialization, however, there are not too many courses within it. The specialization starts off with covering The First Step in Entrepreneurship and continues on with discussing Idea to Marketplace and Startup Funding for Entrepreneurs. Lastly, there is an entrepreneurship capstone. Check this specialization out today as well!

The above courses and specializations do not have to be taken in any particular order. However, please be aware that many of these courses do have specific dates in which they run. Start going on Coursera, Udemy, Codecademy and many more sites today, and start developing key skills to become an excellent entrepreneur. Also, please be aware that it is possible some of these courses may not be offered anymore. Chances are there should be some sort of archive located somewhere though.

CHAPTER 10

Creativity & Follow-Through

EVER WONDER HOW you can become more creative? Ever had an idea? If you answered yes to both of these questions, then it is possible for you to expand upon your creativity. Perhaps one of the most obvious ways to become more creative and come up with more ideas, is through writing down ALL of your ideas. Many of you might be saying to yourself, "Not all the ideas I come up with are good, do I still write them down?" The answer is YES! Writing them down helps you continuously come up with new ones. Some of those ideas might be duds, but the more you write them down, the chances increase of you jotting down a great one someday (like most things, getting the right idea is often a numbers game).

Keep A Journal

About a year or two ago, I began writing down all of the ideas that I had every day. Some days I would write down about four or five and other days I might have wrote down no ideas at all. The number that I would come up with in a given day certainly fluctuated (which is okay). I keep all of my ideas in a journal and if for some reason I do not have it, I choose to jot down ideas on a scrap piece of paper, put it in my pocket, and transfer it into the journal at a later time (this is very important). I urge everyone to use a journal or a notebook to keep all of your ideas in. It's important to at least do this to record your "initial" thoughts. If you want to utilize something else to start going into more detail, then feel free to use what you would like at that point (Ex. computer, smartphone, tablet, etc.). The more that you write down your ideas, the more you will begin thinking "outside-the-box." I really surprised myself with how many I was coming up with when I continuously began writing them all down.

Sticking With It

Like most things, it is important to note that you should "stick with it." Do not slack and not write down any ideas for days at a time (unless truly none come to mind). There was a time when I slacked in regards to writing down new ideas for a few days, and then a few days became a week or two. At that point, you can almost feel yourself not being as creative as you probably would have been if you stuck with writing down all your ideas. Remember, repetition is key! If you want to have a nice free throw shot in basketball, what do you do? You stand in front of a hoop and take shot after shot (repetition) until the shot is as close to perfection as possible (because nothing is truly perfect). Once I began writing down ALL of my ideas again, I noticed my creativity began to rise once more.

Follow-Through

Here's another basketball analogy: If you want to ensure the basket will go in the hoop, how can you increase the probability that it will go in? One of the acceptable answers is "you follow-through." Do not just write down all of your ideas and just leave them sitting in your notebook. Be sure to take a look at them (the duds and the intriguing ones) and sift through them a few times per week, month or year. Place a star next to the ones that seem like they could become something special. If placing a star next to the good ideas is of no interest to you, then highlight them (do whatever you want to distinguish those ideas as the best ideas in your journal). After you sift through many of them, take a look at the good ones and sift through them again at some point. Pick three to five of the best ones and start heavily looking into them. If they resemble an idea that is already out there, then market research will probably be one of the next steps. However, if after researching an idea, it seems like it is very unique, it is probably time to start doing some idea validation (follow the lean startup method).

Ideas are great. I personally believe that we need more of them in the world. If Steve Jobs, Elon Musk and Bill Gates did not come up with many brilliant ideas and "follow-through" with them, where would the world be today? I do not even want to think about that question. Start writing down more ideas today and increase your creativity and volume.

Lean Thinking Makes Ideas Possible

A while back I read the book "The Lean Startup" by Eric Ries. In the book, Ries discusses the process of lean thinking and how it should be applied when developing a startup company. In order to make sense of this lean thinking methodology, one needs to understand first what a startup is, based upon the definition Ries gives in his book. According to Ries, "A startup is a human institution designed to deliver a new product or service under conditions of extreme uncertainty." This definition really interested me, partly because it can even apply to large enterprises looking to develop a new product or service.

Applying Lean Thinking

After learning a little about lean thinking through reading the book, I became interested in learning even more about it, by seeing what the internet had to offer. I began researching to learn more about lean thinking and found some interesting examples and descriptions. There was definitely good information out there, but still, nothing compared to what Ries discussed throughout his book. There is a process that goes with lean thinking, but a simplified way of looking at it, could be as follows:

- Having an idea
- Developing assumptions
- Idea validation
- Creating an MVP (Minimum-Viable-Product)
- Testing the MVP
- Adapting to meet the biggest needs of customers
- Developing a final product

Some people may disagree and think that this simplified way of looking at lean thinking is incorrect, but visualizing lean thinking in this light has helped me to quickly understand what Ries was beginning to touch upon at the start of his book. It truly makes sense to take an idea that you have, and then develop some assumptions around it (since market research is really only an option if there is certainty surrounding an idea). Then comes idea validation, which helps to see if 1. Your assumptions are correct or 2. Your assumptions are off and need to change. Next, comes the creation of the "MVP" which is essentially a product or service that can be created in an almost "bare-bone minimum" capacity. This product or service is meant to be changed several times, to adapt to what customers are truly looking for. A series of tests will surround the MVP and negative feedback is OKAY – as long as it is used to improve upon the product or service. It is important when utilizing lean thinking to remember that this process is great because it can often save time and money – instead of just jumping into business with an idea that you personally think is good (idea validation is key). One of the next steps in the process is to take a look at the needs of customers and develop a "final" product or service that you know they will use (final, is a very open term here since it is likely that the product or service would have many more revisions over the course of time).

Examples of Lean Thinking (Lean Startup Model)

A good example of lean thinking is Facebook. Mark Zuckerberg, co-founder of Facebook, executed a perfect lean mindset when developing the company. A timeline of the steps that he took, look somewhat like this:

- Zuckerberg noticed a need for online social interaction amongst people and college campuses.
- He developed an MVP that was very simple and did not have too many features (aka "the profile page").
- Some people became early adopters of it (a few college campuses).
- The platform was tested by many users and quickly became popular (it began going viral).
- Zuckerberg and company continued to make adjusts to the site, and continue to do so today to meet the needs of their user base.

The example above is essentially a quick timeline of how I believe Facebook utilized a lean way of thinking when it came to developing its platform. One of the biggest benefits of lean thinking, is that there is often less risk versus just running with an idea with minimal or no validation. Listen to your users or customers (as I mentioned before) – validation is key!

I still have a lot to learn when it comes to the lean startup (lean thinking) methodology, but I will say that the more I discuss this mindset with people, the more I love it. I think every entrepreneur, student, parent or business should take a look at applying this mindset because of how powerful it can be. Since I began utilizing a more lean way of thinking, my creativity has skyrocketed. Ideas that I might have brushed off in the past, began to become more of a reality if I were to use a lean approach. Everyone should definitely pick up a copy of "The Lean Startup" by Eric Ries (if you haven't already done so) and begin utilizing the lean mindset today!

CHAPTER 11

Motivation Is Key

I AM A big believer in finding constant motivation. Some of the best ways to find motivation can be through books, movies, television shows and music. I thought for the purpose of the book, it would be a good idea to include some popular motivational resources for you to utilize (in no particular order):

Books

- "Think and Grow Rich" by Napoleon Hill
- "Be Obsessed or Be Average" by Grant Cardone
- "Tony Robbins Greatest Life Lessons" by Joy Lincoln
- "The Millionaire Fastlane: Crack the Code to Wealth and Live Rich for a Lifetime!" by M.J. DeMarco
- "The Art of Exceptional Living" by Jim Rohn
- "Creativity, Inc.: Overcoming the Unseen Forces That Stand in the Way of True Inspiration" by Ed Catmull

- "The Millionaire Mind" by Thomas J. Stanley
- "Awaken the Giant Within: How to Take Immediate Control of Your Mental, Emotional, Physical and Financial Destiny!" by Tony Robbins
- "I Will Teach You To Be Rich" by Ramit Sethi
- "Switch: How to Change Things When Change Is Hard" by Chip Heath
- "The $100 Startup" by Chris Guillebeau
- "Emotional Intelligence 2.0" by Travis Bradberry & Jean Greaves

Some of the above books, I have read and others are currently on my reading list. If you are interested in seeing the books that I have read, the ones I am currently reading, and the ones that I want to read; please check out my Goodreads account using the following link: https://www.goodreads.com/review/list/48250459. Lately, I have been on a mission to read at least one book per week, and so far have stuck true to my goal. When you think about it, reading one book per week is not that hard. Let's say the average book has two-hundred and fifty words in it, which would mean you would have to read approximately thirty-six pages per day (not hard at all). Bring your book wherever you go, and read when you have a few minutes (remember, every minute counts).

I tend to gravitate more towards books that have to do with success, business, finance or entrepreneurship, because those are topics that genuinely interest me. The books above are great resources to find motivation through reading, and are only a few of the many good motivational books that are out there. I won't discuss the reasoning behind all that I included in the list, but I will talk about "Think and Grow Rich" by Napoleon Hill. This is one of those books that has the ability to change your life. Think I'm kidding? Read it. I read it in a week and fell in love with its contents. Napoleon Hill goes beyond where the typical author goes, and inspires readers in such a profound way. Once I started reading it, I could not put it down. In the book, Hill discusses a lot about how to obtain money, but he does it in a way that is centered on having the right "mindset." Good habits, the right thoughts, determination, and education are some of the surest ways to inch towards success. This book is one that I believe every freshman in high school should be given when they step through the door. Along with some of the "handouts" the government provides, this book should also be given to people on welfare. I bet if the government took this initiative, the number of people on welfare would drop over time. If inspiration is what you seek, then please look no further than "Think and Grow Rich." It will change your life!

Movies & TV Shows

Below are some movies and television shows that I highly recommend current or aspiring entrepreneurs watch (if and when they have any free time). I am not a big fan of wasting time watching movies or television shows anymore, but I always make an exception when I have the chance to watch any of these:

Movies

- The Social Network (2010)
- The Wolf of Wall Street (2013)
- The Pursuit of Happyness (2006)
- Wall Street: Money Never Sleeps (2010)
- The Aviator (2004)
- The Great Gatsby (2013)

There is somewhat of a pattern with these movies:

1. They all feature famous actors: Jesse Eisenberg, Leonardo DiCaprio, Will Smith, Michael Douglas, etc.
2. They are all motivational.
3. The main characters face problems throughout the film.
4. Despite the struggles, the main characters in the films find ways to overcome them (with

the exception of Jordan Belfort in the Wolf of Wall Street).

A lot of you might be wondering why I included "The Great Gatsby" on my list. This movie is great because it shows a wealthy man "living the life." He has all the fancy cars, an exceptional house and so many friends wanting to be with him every day. It is meant to inspire you to strive for a great life one day. For those reasons, I feel it deserves to be on this list. After watching any of these movies, I typically become even more motivated than I was before, and am recharged and ready to get to work right away. Check out any of these today (even if you have already seen them). There is always room for more motivation in your life!

Television Shows

- The Profit
- Shark Tank
- Restaurant Startup
- Blue Collar Millionaires
- Make Me A Millionaire Inventor

This is not a subtle way of promoting CNBC. All of these shows are on CNBC, but that is only because when it comes to business this channel trumps all others (in my opinion). CNBC really made it a point years ago to have business-related programs playing all the time. Many of these you have probably heard of, but I am sure there are a couple up there that you have not watched before. The Profit is my absolute favorite show. It features Marcus Lemonis, a savvy investor and entrepreneur (who also happens to be one of my idols) that takes his own money and invests it in small businesses. Marcus goes through the process of what a good business needs and frequently utilizes his three keys to success for any business: People, Product, and Process. Typically, Marcus will only invest in businesses that have at least good people and a good product. The process is something he feels is fixable (in most cases).

I have mentioned it before, but feel it is important to mention once again, the fact that I tend to include many business-centered ideas in this book. Even if you know you are not into business, it still does not hurt to learn more about it, since it is all around you. Open your mind to becoming more entrepreneurial so that one day you can run your own business if you want to!

Music

- "Till I Collapse" by Eminem

"This is your moment and every single minute you spend trying to hold onto it cause you may never get it again."

- "Remember the name" - Fort Minor

"This is ten percent luck, Twenty percent skill, Fifteen percent concentrated power of will, Five percent pleasure, Fifty percent pain, And a hundred percent reason to remember the name."

- "Lose Yourself" by Eminem

"You only get one shot, do not miss your chance to blow, This opportunity comes once in a lifetime."

- "You Raise Me Up" by Josh Groban (not a pump-up song, but very motivational)

"There is no life, no life without its hunger, Each restless heart beats so imperfectly, But then you come, and I am filled with wonder, Sometimes I think I glimpse eternity."

There are many more motivational and pump-up songs than this. I just wanted to give you a little taste of what some of my favorite are. Also, be sure to look up pump up songs, because those often work best to get you "fired up!"

Real Life Motivation

I am sure there are many of you out there that make up excuses why you can't be rich and successful one day.

Whether it has to do with your parents, the way you were raised, your current living situation or the bogus other excuses you tell yourself on a daily basis; the point is that none of that should define your future success. YOU CAN DO WHATEVER YOU SET YOUR MIND TO! I sometimes get into disagreements with people who disagree with me when I say "anyone can become a millionaire." People also say back to me that "if it's so easy to become a millionaire, why aren't you one?" First of all, I never said that attaining a net worth of million dollars is anywhere close to easy. However, I believe I will be a millionaire one day because of MY MINDSET. I have worked hard to get where I am today and I will continue to work even harder to make my first million. The truth of the matter is anyone can actually become a millionaire one day, but the path to get there may be much tougher for some. Attaining high amounts of wealth has to do with a person's drive, plan, persistence, and willpower. Ignore the haters and surround yourself with more positive people. For those of you that still think certain people do not have the opportunity to become a million, I thought it would be a good idea to include a few examples of individuals that have conquered the odds and become very wealthy and successful.

John Paul DeJoria

Many of you probably don't know who John Paul DeJoria is, but there is a good chance you have heard of two of the companies he has started: John Paul Mitchell Systems and Patron Tequila. In 2016, DeJoria was believed to have a net worth of approximately three billion dollars. He was not always this wealthy, though. Growing up, DeJoria ended up living in a foster home and was also part of a gang for a while before joining the military. Using a seven hundred dollar loan, he created John Paul Mitchell Systems and began selling shampoo house-to-house, all while living in his car at the time.[1]

Do Won Chang

Do Won Chang is the founder of the popular clothing store, Forever 21. In 1981, Chang and his wife moved from Korea to the United States. Chang worked as a janitor, gas station attendant and in a coffee shop at the same time in order to make enough money to live. He and his wife later opened their first store in 1984 and it has been all uphill since then. Today, Chang has a net worth of close to three billion dollars. [1](Baer, Drake. "14 Billionaires Who Started With Nothing..." Business Insider. 29 Sept. 2014. Web)

Tony Robbins

The man, the myth, the legend. Tony Robbins is one of the most prolific motivational speakers, philanthropists, and all-around gurus the world has ever come across (my opinion is easy to tell here). Robbins has an estimated net worth of almost five-hundred million dollars. He was yet another successful and wealthy individual that grew up facing some adversity. In one interview, Robbins discussed how when he was only seventeen years old, his mother chased him out of the house with a knife. On top of that, he mentioned how he was physically abused by his mother when he was only a child. However, rather than mope around and think he received the short end of the stick of this thing we call life, he turned it around and became massively successful. Here's a great quote that show's his mindset: "Our worst challenges, our worst problems, our worst failures — for those who don't give up — they give you insights." (Little, Katie. "How Tony Robbins Rebounded from an Abusive Childhood..." CNBC. 27 June 2016. Web.)

There are many more examples of people who are wildly successful today but started out with not the best life. You are in control of your destiny and as long as you stay positive, persistent, and try to separate yourself from negative people; you will put yourself on a much better path towards success!

Quotes

I feel it is very important for individuals to have favorite quotes. Here are some of my favorite ones:

- “In order to be successful, you have to make sure that being rejected doesn’t bother you at all.” - Bill Ackman
- “Some people want it to happen, some wish it would happen, others make it happen.” - Michael Jordan
- “There’s a way to do it better - find it.” - Thomas Edison
- “A positive mind finds a way it can be done; a negative mind looks for all the ways it can’t be done.” - Napoleon Hill
- “I don’t have time is the biggest lie you tell yourself.” - Grant Cardone
- “Everything you’ve ever wanted is on the other side of fear.” - George Adair
- “Opportunities don’t happen, you create them.” - Chris Grosser
- “What you do today can improve all your tomorrows.” - Ralph Marston

Find quotes that can motivate you. Every time I read the quotes that I have posted above, I begin to feel inspired. Quotes can be very powerful and should be used often. If you find one that you are very passionate about, write it down and carry it with you or perhaps post in on your LinkedIn or Twitter account (assuming you have one). Seeing a quote often will allow you to really take it to heart, and produce self-motivation on more of a daily basis.

Appendix: Useful Resources

I thought it would be a good idea to include all of the useful resources (a sort-of MEGA GUIDE) that I have either used or heard about throughout my life thus far. There are many great websites and tools out there for students and people of all ages to use, that can benefit their life drastically. Each resource has been separated into different categories for your viewing. Enjoy!

Education-related

- www.coursera.com - "1000+ courses from schools like Stanford and Yale - no application required"
- www.khanacademy.com - "expert-created content and resources for every subject and level"
- www.udemy.com - "online learning and teaching marketplace with over 40,000 courses and 13 million students"
- www.codecademy.com - "interactive courses on how to program"
- www.edx.org - "free online courses from the world's best universities"
- www.wallstreetprep.com - "financial modeling self-study courses and instructor-led financial modeling training"

- www.alison.com - "provider of free online classes & online learning"
- iTunes U - "complete courses from leading universities and other schools"
- www.ocw.mit.edu - "web-based publication of virtually all MIT course content"
- www.ted.com - "influential videos from expert speakers on education, business, science, tech and creativity"
- www.duolingo.com - "world's most popular way to learn a language"
- www.skillshare.com - "online education platform with classes taught by the world's best practitioners"
- www.youtube.com - "enjoy the videos and music you love, upload original content"
- www.freecodecamp.com - "learn to code and build projects for nonprofit"
- www.datamonkey.pro - "learn to analyze data"
- www.memrise.com - "uses images and science to make learning easy and fun"
- www.dough.com - "the next generation of investment software designed to make trading options simple and fun"
- www.wealthlift.com - "an easy way to learn how to invest"
- www.guides.co - "free publishing and hosting platform for sharing the world's information"

- www.yousician.com - "the fast, fun way to learn, play and master the piano, guitar, bass or ukulele"
- www.pianu.com - "new way to learn piano, online, interactively, using a real keyboard"
- www.chesscademy.com - "learn how to play chess online through videos, chess tactics, and chess games"

News-related

- www.techcrunch.com - "a leading technology media property, dedicated to obsessively profiling startups, reviewing new Internet products, and breaking tech news"
- www.cnet.com - "leader in tech product reviews, news, prices, videos, forums, how-tos and more"
- www.engadget.com - "a web magazine with obsessive daily coverage of everything new in gadgets and consumer electronics"
- www.seekingalpha.com - "stock market insights & financial analysis, including free earnings call transcripts, investment ideas and ETF & stock research written by finance experts"
- www.thestreet.com - "get business news that moves markets, award-winning stock analysis, market data and stock trading ideas"

- www.huffingtonpost.com - "offering coverage of US politics, entertainment, style, world news, technology and comedy"
- www.washingtonpost.com - "breaking news and analysis on politics, business, world national news, entertainment and more"
- www.wsj.com - "coverage of breaking news and current headlines from the US and around the world"
- www.forbes.com - "business news and financial news"
- www.ft.com - "international business news, analysis, market data and company information"

Entrepreneurship-related

- www.entrepreneur.com - "advice, insight, profiles and guides for established and aspiring entrepreneurs worldwide"
- www.inc.com - "get advice, tools, and services that help your small business grow"
- www.fastcompany.com - "inspires a new breed of innovative and creative thought leaders who are actively inventing the future of business"
- www.cnbc.com - "get latest business news on stock markets, financial & earnings on CNBC"

- www.startupstash.com - "a curated directory of resources and tools to help you build your startup"
- www.angel.co - "where the world meets startups. Find a great startup job, invest in a startup, or raise money"
- www.startupcompanylawyer.com - "comprehensive list of startup lawyer posts"
- www.crunchbase.com - "the leading platform to discover innovative companies and the people behind them"
- www.mixergy.com - "startup stories with 1000+ entrepreneurs"
- www.score.org - "free small business advice"
- www.sba.gov - "electronic gateway of procurement information for and about small businesses"
- www.franchise.org - "information on franchising, selecting a franchise, financing and starting a franchise"
- www.bizbuysell.com - "listings of business opportunities and resources to assist with buying and selling"
- www.incorporate.com - "protect your assets by forming an LLC or incorporating online today"
- www.venturebeat.com - "leading source for news & perspective on tech innovation"

- www.irs.gov - "the U.S. government agency responsible for tax collection and tax law enforcement"
- www.buyerzone.com - "get expert buying advice and price quotes on 100+ business products"
- www.vistaprint.com - "empowers you to design and customize affordable marketing materials for your business"
- www.wix.com - "customize with a free website builder, no coding skills needed. Choose a design, begin customizing and be online today"
- www.dropbox.com - "secure file sharing and storage"
- www.trello.com - "web-based project management application"
- www.stripe.com - "a suite of APIs that powers commerce for businesses of all sizes"
- www.createspace.com - "provides free tools to help you self-publish and distribute your books, DVDs, CDs, and video downloads on-demand on Amazon.com and other sites"
- www.thegamecrafter.com - "users can upload their artwork and then have their board game assembled"
- www.newspaperclub.com - "we are here to help everyone make their own newspaper. Print one copy or thousands, from a range of sizes. We ship internationally"

- www.alibaba.com - "find quality manufacturers, suppliers, exporters, importers, buyers, wholesalers, products and trade leads from our award-winning international trade site"
- www.strikingly.com - "the best website builder for anyone to build a gorgeous, mobile-friendly website easily"
- www.docracy.com - "the web's only open collection of legal contracts and the best way to negotiate and sign documents online"
- www.producthunt.com - "is a curation of the best new products, every day"
- www.kickstarter.com - "the world's largest funding platform for creative projects"
- www.mailchimp.com - "online email marketing solution to manage subscribers, send emails, and track results"
- www.buffer.com - "a smarter way to share on social media"
- www.slack.com - "brings all your communication together in one place. It's real-time messaging, archiving and search for modern teams"
- www.typeform.com - "build beautiful, engaging, and conversational online forms, surveys, quizzes, landing pages, and much more"

Investment-related

- www.investopedia.com - "the world's leading source of financial content on the web, ranging from market news to retirement strategies, investing education to insights"
- www.finance.yahoo.com - "you get free stock quotes, up-to-date news, portfolio management resources, international market data, social interaction and mortgage rates"
- www.fool.com - "provides leading insight and analysis about stocks, helping investors stay informed"
- www.finviz.com - "stock screener for investors and traders, financial visualizations"
- www.stocktouch.com - "tells you more in five seconds than you would learn reading financial news all day"
- www.robinhood.com - "free stock trading. Stop paying up to $10 for every trade"
- www.betterment.com - "is the smarter automated investing service that provides optimized investment returns for individual, IRA, Roth IRA & rollover 401(k) accounts"
- www.wealthfront.com - "manages your investments for you online. We personalize, diversify, rebalance low-fee Individual, IRA, Roth IRA & 401(k) rollover accounts"

- www.openfolio.com - "don't invest alone. Leverage the knowledge of over 70,000 real investors and start investing better, together"
- www.feex.com - "FeeX takes care of the hard work of rolling over your old 401k for you"
- www.estimize.com - "earnings and economic estimates contributed by the entire financial community, with a powerful predictive analytics layer"
- www.stocktwits.com - "financial communications platform for the investing community. Learn from other stock traders and get new ideas"
- www.acorns.com - "Acorns automatically invests your spare change"
- www.thinkorswim.com - "trade w/ advanced trading tools"
- www.forcerank.com - "boils the stock market down to a single question: will stock ABC outperform stock XYZ this week?"
- www.tdameritrade.com - "online broker for online stock trading, long-term investing, and retirement planning"
- www.stockcharts.com - "award-winning charting tools, analysis resources and expert commentary you need to invest"

- www.google.com/finance - "get real-time stock quotes & charts, financial news, currency conversions, or track your portfolio"
- www.biggerpockets.com - "social network for the real estate investing community. Learn real estate investment, get free tips & education, make deals, and grow your business"
- www.realtor.com - "search real estate property records, houses, condos, land and more"
- www.loopnet.com - "search commercial real estate for sale and lease. Find your next investment property, office space, land or industrial space"
- www.auction.com - "the nation's leading online marketplace for buying and selling real estate"
- www.realtymogul.com - "an online marketplace offering crowdfunding for real estate investing opportunities"
- www.lendingclub.com - "America's #1 credit marketplace"

Job-related

- www.indeed.com - "find millions of jobs from thousands of company web sites, job boards and newspapers"
- www.glassdoor.com - "find a job and company you love. Reviews, salaries and benefits from

employees. Interview questions from candidates. Millions of jobs"

- www.upwork.com - "find freelancers and freelance jobs"
- www.toptal.com - "enables start-ups, businesses, and organizations to hire freelancers from a growing network of the best custom software developers and designers"
- www.workingnomads.co - "curated list of remote jobs, for the modern working nomad"
- www.jobpspresso.co - "easiest way to find remote jobs, careers and other remote work opportunities at interesting and innovative companies"
- www.f6s.com - "thousands of startup job vacancies at top startups"
- www.hired.com - "create a profile & vetted companies compete for you, reaching out with salary & equity upfront"
- www.roberthalf.com - "provides professional staffing services in a variety of industries"

College-related

- www.careeronestop.com - "learn about careers, find career information, and locate career resources and advice"
- www.collegetransfer.net - "college transfer simplified"

- www.simpletuition.com - "find student loans to pay for college or refinance existing college debt"
- www.alltuition.com - "free and fast unified application for college financial aid"
- www.collegeboard.org - "find official college planning and preparation tools to help you succeed
- www.careercolleges.com - "a directory of online and campus based career colleges and offers a career assessment test to help guide your career search"
- www.cheapesttextbooks.com - "find the cheapest place to buy used textbooks, new textbooks, rental textbooks"
- www.studentrate.com - "free student discounts and deals on Apple, Netflix, T-Mobile, Sephora, Forever 21 and much more"
- www.quizlet.com - "makes simple learning tools that let you study anything. Start learning today with flashcards, games and learning tools"
- www.wolframalpha.com - "a search engine that gives you access to the world's facts and data and calculates answers across a range of topics"
- www.unigo.com - "read college reviews, get matched to schools, find scholarships, and more"

- www.collegetips.com - "online college survival guide that contains tips and advice for high school and college students"
- www.goabroad.com - "directory guide for study abroad, language schools, internships, and international volunteer positions"
- www.thecollegeinvestor.com - "a personal finance and investing blog focused on helping millennials escape student loan debt and start building wealth"
- www.yourfreecareertest.com - "career test free for high school & college students"
- www.internships.com - "find internships and employment opportunities in the largest internship marketplace. Search paid internships and part time jobs to help start your career"
- www.studentloanhero.com - "calculators and tools to pay off student loans"
- www.ratemyprofessor.com - "review teachers and professors"
- www.smallpdf.com - "the platform that makes it super easy to convert and edit all your PDF files"
- www.collegetransfer.net - "Will my courses transfer? What about changing majors? Can I get in? What will it cost? How long will it take? Where to go?"

- www.transferology.com - "shows how courses you have taken or plan to take transfer to another ... Simply enter your courses to find equivalent courses at other schools"

...and many more.

As you can see there are many resources out there that can help you along your journey. This list is certainly not all the tools and sites that you can use, but it's a great guide. I advise everyone to look through each of these and find out which you would like to use to help you in your quest for a successful future.

Closing Remarks

I hope you enjoyed what the book had to offer. It was really fun putting it together and being able to write about a topic that is very close to my heart. Planning for your future is so important and it is something I feel many people "miss the boat on." I think it's also important to live in the moment, but only if you have peace of mind when it comes to what your plan for the future may look like. On top of writing about this topic, I also provide consulting services and speeches when requested. If you are interested in learning more about me or these offerings, please be sure to check out my website – www.jaredstaylor.com and follow me on Twitter & Instagram @jaredstaylor.

Thanks!

- Jared Taylor

www.ingramcontent.com/pod-product-compliance
Lightning Source LLC
Chambersburg PA
CBHW031323040426
42443CB00005B/191
9780692846179